"GOOD MORNING LADYWOOD"

Mac Joseph

Front cover: The Old Steam Clock, Morville Street, Ladywood, Birmingham

Back Cover: St. Barnabas' Church, Ryland Street, Ladywood, Birmingham

Typeset, Printed and Published by M. D. Joseph, Stafford

First printed in October 1999

ISBN 0 9537038 0 0

Contents

Introduction 1

Foreword 2

Ladywood Road 3

Monument Road 11

Morville Street 25

St. Vincent Street and Gilby Road 31

Ledsam Street 37

Ruston Street 43

Hickman's 49

Landon's 53

Entertainment 57

Schools 71

Summerfield Swimming Club 83

Memories 87

Around the Area 103

"GOOD MORNING, LADYWOOD"

It was several years ago that I decided to write a book about Ladywood, but the book had to be different and I wanted to include the memories and photographs of the real people of the area, hopefully, I have succeeded.

I was born in Morville Street in 1948 and lived with my parents Ron and Freda Joseph at number 64.

My grandparents, George and Edith Compton lived at 1/57 Morville Street, which was a small terrace house with the brewhouse at the bottom of the yard. My other aunts and uncles lived in Ruston Street and Shakespeare Road as well as Morville Street.

Apart from one period, I lived in Ladywood until 1969 in Monument Road, Elizabeth Fry House and Marroway Street. I then married Pauline, who lived in Gilby Road and we moved to Gorsy Road, Quinton.

The greatest challenge was in locating photographs from the area, but people have been generous in loaning me their treasured memories and I thank them.

Please enjoy this trip down Memory Lane.

Mac Joseph

I would like to dedicate this book

To my wife, Pauline and son Andrew

FOREWORD

Malcolm David Joseph, but Mac to everyone who really knows him.

Mac and I met after he had heard me on one of my many chats on Radio WM with another dear friend of ours, Dr. Carl Chinn, about two years ago.

With a name like Mac, one would immediately think of Scotland, but then David and that takes you to Wales, which is where his dad originated.

Mac was born in Morville Street, Ladywood, Birmingham, and a place never to be forgotten by him. It was the comfort, love and security of these early years that prompted him to use his deep fondness and urgent desire to do something for Ladywood past.

Hard and long research visits to people who lived in Ladywood in those hard post war times, collecting information and photographs. Carefully copied, and returned trustingly to these people who had generously loaned these precious items to him.

The title Mac chose for this walk down the streets of yesteryear is **"GOOD MORNING, LADYWOOD"** certainly gets one off on an early journey through the wonderful history of this area.

To open this book is alike to opening a fresh caught oyster and finding the most precious pearl the world has ever seen.

The respect and admiration I have for Mac makes me feel honoured to regard him as a friend.

Ron "Smudge" Smith

Ladywood Road

LADYWOOD

LADYWOOD ROAD

Looking from Islington Row towards Ladywood Road

Ambulance Station (left) and Police Station (right)

THE ALMSHOUSES

The almshouses were built for Lench's Trust in 1859. They are situated at the top of Ladywood Road, near Five Ways. The land was purchased for the princely sum of £1200. The name Lench derives from William Lench, a tanner from Moor Street. The Almshouses are built in a quadrangle and occupy two floors.

To be eligible for admission to the Almshouses an applicant had to be a poor woman, spinster or widow (only women were allowed to enter) of good character and have resided in Birmingham for more than 5 years. The rules for residents were quite simple: they were not allowed out after 10 p.m. and the bailiff's permission was required to go away at all. A certain amount of their own furniture was allowed and stipend of 10s. 6d. plus an allowance for coal per week.

There were already 3 other Almshouses in Birmingham, at Hospital Street, Conybere Street and Ravenhurst Street and the Ladywood site became the showpiece of the Trust.

The inscription above the two side wings reads: *"Lench's Trust, Almshouses, erected MDCCCCLIX, Charles Clifford, Esq., Bailiff of the Charity"* on the left side; and *"Lench's Trust, Almshouses, erected MDCCCLIX,   Arthur Byland, Bailiff of the Charity"* on the right hand side.

The old dwarfed by the new

LADYWOOD SOCIAL CLUB

The Ladywood Social Club provides amenities for local people who enjoy a pleasant night out.

The Club provides facilities for a quiet drink, concerts, dances and bingo.

Trips are also arranged for the elderly members of the Club. The Club was originally located in Monument Road.

The new Club was opened in October 1971 and is located on the Ladywood Middleway, next to the Police Station.

The Eagle and Ball corner of Morville Street and Ladywood Road

The Opening of Ladywood Police Station, November 1966

J. W. Hanley & Son, Butcher, 122 Ladywood Road

Two spinsters, Misses Wails, who did dressmaking and alterations. On the corner there was a sweet shop, continuing down from Five Ways you reached:

- Eagle and Ball
- Matthews
- Fruit and Veg shop
- Arnolds
- Beryls
- Wheelers
- Milletts
- Furbers
- Millies
- Post Office.
- Bank
- Franks the hairdresser
- Sweet shop
- Almshouses
- Ladywood Police Station
- Children's Hospital.

Beaufort Garage opposite Beaufort Road

Fire at the corner of Alston Street, August 1973

View showing Wood Street, taken from Wells Tower

Monument Road

LADYWOOD

MONUMENT ROAD

Monument Road ran from Hagley Road to Spring Hill Library, the road contained a variety of shops, entertainment, banks, churches and a health centre.

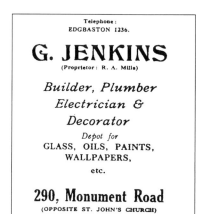

The Nags Head on the corner of Icknield Port Road
and Monument Road

Pearks on the corner of Wood Street and
Monument Road

LLOYDS BANK IN LADYWOOD

1894 - Lloyds Bank open a sub-branch to Edgbaston, known as Ladywood, in shop premises

1897 - Ladywood becomes a branch

1904 - Branch moves to new purpose built premises at 328 Monument Road

1961 - 27 February branch moves to new premises at 187 Hagley Road, and name changes to Ivy Bush Branch

1986 - Through-the-wall cashpoint is installed at the branch

1987 - Branch reverts to sub-branch status under Edgbaston branch

1992 - Branch Closes

60th Anniversary of the Bank

The history of Lloyds in Ladywood can be traced back to 1894 when a sub-branch was opened under the supervision of the Manager of the Edgbaston branch of the Bank. Three years later, however, the office as raised to the status of a full branch.. Ladywood at the turn of the century had lost much of the character, which gave it its picturesque name. There dwelt the wealthy manufacturers to whom the motor car was a novelty and who were later, through it said and influence, to move to newer and more distant suburbs leaving industry the predominant feature.

The branch was originally housed in shop premises, but a new building at 328 Monument Road was erected in 1904 and the business transferred. Few people will remember the hoarding surrounding the land on which the new premises were being constructed with its big recruiting poster featuring Bugler Dunne who was killed at Colenso. The first occupant of the Bank House was a Mr. Ramsden who was private secretary to Mr. Howard Lloyd, General Manager of the Bank from 1871 until 1902.

Lloyds Bank at Five Ways, Edgbaston

MONUMENT ROAD BATHS

The Baths were opened in 1883, by the then Mayor Councillor White, amid controversy about the site and cost of £20,000.

They were built in the street and on the site of Icene, and no doubt many a Roman Legion passed up and down the road many a time.

Many an Olympic candidate used the baths for training.

Sadly, the Baths have now been demolished

Left: the entrance to the baths on Monument Road

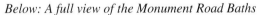

Below: A full view of the Monument Road Baths

An early postcard of Monument Road

Monument Road showing Canny's and Betty's

The Bridge Inn on the corner of Ledsam Street

Monument Road showing Hickman's

Monument Road showing Landon's Bathroom shop

The Welfare Centre in Monument Road

LES-RAY HAIRDRESSER'S

Les-Ray Gentlemen's Hairdressers occupied the premises of 375 Monument Road, Ladywood. There were two doors at the front, one for the shop and the other for the residents who lived there, Ron and Freda Joseph and their son, Malcolm. The living accommodation comprised of hall, lounge, kitchen, and two bedrooms upstairs, then up more stairs to an attic with a small room off with a sky light. Les-Ray was Les Jeavons and Ray James who occupied the shop from 1957-1962 (the previous owner was Mr. Sadler).

The shop in Monument Road, only two doors away from the Station Inn

Originally Les and Ray worked for a man called Mr. Weaver in Hay Mills and one day they were talking and Ray said he would like to have a crack on his own, Les said he would as well, that's where the Monument Road shop started.

Back to Monument Road - they had decided to have a go at a shop in Kings Heath, then one night Ron Joseph went to see Ray at his house on the Coventry Road and asked Ray to run the Monument Road shop for him. Les and Ray went to the chap who had the shop and during the conversation he said *"you'd be surprised the number of people that pass here"*. Those words became very significant later, because they took the shop over in the February, a bad month for barbers, being cold etc. and considering it had only been a been a one-man shop for years, they both had to make a living out it.

The number of times, over the next few months, they stood in the doorway inside the salon, when people were coming out of the factories at 5 o'clock, that Les and Ray repeated those words *"You'd be surprised how many people pass here"*. Anyway, over the next few month's things improved and they started making a living out it. But they still couldn't get any stock for the shelves, Brylcreem etc. It looked barren so they used to put empty cigarette packets on the shelf, then eventually they found a warehouse, Ellison's, who supplied them with goods and from there on they dealt with no one but Ellison's.

When the shop was up and running they decided to expand with another shop, this time in Rookery Road, Handsworth. They then employed another barber who worked in the

Monument Road shop and Ray went up to the Rookery Road shop. Then in a short space of time they employed another person up there.

Then came the shop in Granville Street. Rya saw it advertised in the Mail and he knew it would be a good thing, even though it had been closed for a few weeks. An old chap called Morris who lived close to Ray on the Coventry Road owned it. After Granville Street came Cromwell Street Ladies and Gents, they sold the shop in Rookery Road to help pay for that. Then they had a contract to cut all the lad's hair in Blackwell Open Air School. What a job that was, Les and Ray used to go up there once a month put two chairs in the shower room and cut all the hair. They started at 8.30 and finishing around about 3.00 in the afternoon.

Then came shops in Cregoe Street and Shireland Road. At around this time people started to grow their hair longer and that was the end of their dream of having 12 shops to retire on.

Back to Monument Road, Friday night, busy, shop was full then in walks a customer carrying a shopping bag, no plastic bags in those days, he sat on the chair in the corner. When it was his turn he tried to put this bag on the seat but it fell off and out flew a chicken! This chicken had its legs tied so it couldn't run so what did it do, it flew, absolute chaos. Can you picture it? All the customers, Les and Ray trying to catch this chicken, feathers flying everywhere!

On another day Les and Ray decided to wash the front of the shop, it was such a nice day. So they borrowed a window cleaners wooden ladder. When they came to the part right in front of the entrance to the shop, Les put his foot on the bottom rung of the ladder and one hand on a rung about shoulder height. He intended lowering the ladder by balancing it on the board that Les-Ray is on, but it missed and went straight through the front door window - Panic! Freda, Ron's wife, would be home soon so they had to get the glass in before she came home or she would go mad. Somehow they managed it and they don't think she noticed it for months because nothing was said.

Les used to be a cook during the war so he used to cook the dinner when they first went to Monument Road. He was out their one day when a vicar came in for his haircut it was the first time he had been in the shop. Ray cut his hair and he was nearly finished when he heard a crash from the kitchen, plates being smashed, Les shouting, the door burst open and Les stood there "the ******* cat, I'll wring its neck" and he was going to carry on saying nice things about this cat, when Ray pulled the cloth back off the vicar and Les saw his back to front collar. He stopped in mid sentence stood there with his mouth open and went blood red. Swearing in those days was definitely a "no, no" in front of men of the cloth and females.

Saturday afternoon, a nice day in the summer and the shop was full, except for one chair near the door. A chap walked in, they could see he'd had a few drinks so they ignored him. When it came to his turn he didn't move, so Ray went over to him and shook him, no joy he was fast asleep. OK leave him, next please, then next please and so on until about half an hour before closing, he'd been there for at least 2 hours by this time. Ray said we'd better get him into the chair, so they more or less carried him into the chair for Les to cut his hair, but his head kept falling to one side. Ray had to hold his head up so that Les could finish it and they eventually got it done! Closing time was 6 o'clock and they still couldn't wake him up, so what do they do? Les said that the Station pub had got him into this state so they should have the responsibility, so they frog-marched him up to the Station Inn step and sat him down on that. Well, it was a nice evening wasn't it.

The Church at the lower end of Monument Road, just below the Health Centre

After redevelopment, showing Spring Hill and the Library

21

PALAIS DE DANSE

The Palais was built in 1921 on the corner of Monument Road and Ingleby Street, Ladywood.

The star band was Will Schenkman and his Buffalo Band. One of the famous attractions was the fountain in the centre of the hall. It also had a balcony where you could watch people dancing the waltz, tango and the rumba.

There used to be an evening session and each afternoon a "The Dansant", admission charge was sixpence and included a cup of tea and biscuit.

Many famous bands played the Palais including the great Louis Armstrong, and in 1932, Duke Ellington and his Band.

Most people remember the Palais for its Italian sprung floor. It also had professional dancers, who charged 6d a dance. The Hall had been used for many things in its time, one of them was a menagerie, known locally as the "jungle". On New Year's Eve there would be the appearance of "Old Father Time" and a young girl to symbolise the New Year coming in. The Palais de Danse closed in 1940.

An early postcard advertising the Palais de Danse

Do you remember?

Do you remember?

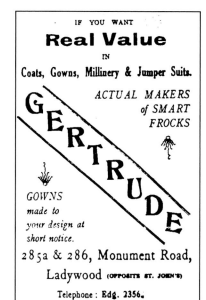

Morville Street

LADYWOOD

MORVILLE STREET

A 1955 map of Morville Street, I lived at 64, and my grandparents at 1/57

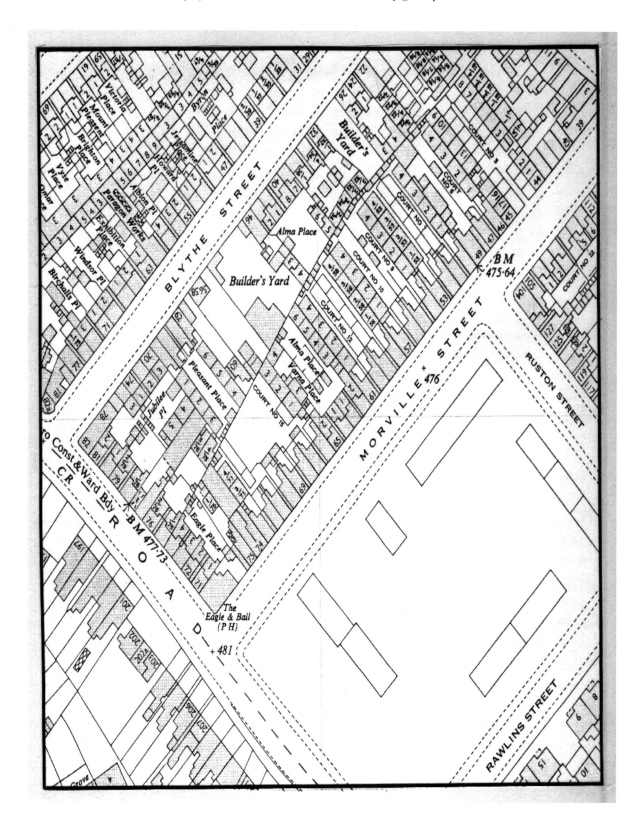

SHOPS AND BUSINESSES - 1933

John Cox, Fish Dealer, 95a Morville Street - You could buy fish and chips for 3d.

A. E. Rose, Shopkeeper, 104 Morville Street - This shop was on the corner of Ruston Street and Morville Street. They sold sweets and they also had sides of bacon   hanging by hooks from the ceiling

Fred Stockton, Newsvendor, 106 Morville Street - This was a house - cum - shop and sold papers, comics at 1/2d each. Enid Blyton books for 1/2d each

Fred Sollors, Dairy, 116 Morville Street

Richard Till, Beer Retailer, 103 Morville Street - Known as "Dickie Tills" and sold beer at 7d. at pint.

The Eagle and Ball, Public House - Licensee in 1933 was Mr. Fred Walters

Bennetts, Confectioners, 70 Morville Street - They sold bread and cottage loaves for 4d.each

The Compton family, George, Edith, Dolly and Freda, in the yard at 1/57 Morville Street

Broadcasting Licence, 1955

The Old Steam Clock, Public House - Doors opened at 7 p.m. for entertainment. Vesta Tilley once appeared here

Wales, Morville Street - Manufactured beds, it was later burnt down

Vernons, Decorators - During the war the yard was used by firewatchers, there was accommodation, and it was turned into a darts room during the blackout for civilians, hopefully not for the firewatchers!

Gilberts, House - cum – shop - Front room was the shop for ladies dresses. Mrs. Gilbert was ill one day, and a note was placed in the window, which read "Please will all drivers drive slowly, ILLNESS"

The Dairy, Morville Street - Sold faggots and peas in a jug, all hot, for 6d. and in the summer 1/2d cream pies.

Above: The Old Steam Clock on the corner of Morville Street and Ledsam Street

Baldwin and Sons, paper bag manufacturers

*The Value
House corner of
Morville Street
and Ruston
Street*

The Eagle and Ball at the corner of Morville Street and Ladywood Road

St. Vincent Street and Gilby Road

LADYWOOD

St. Vincent Street

Looking down St. Vincent Street

Ladywood Supermarket

Looking towards the St. Vincent Public House

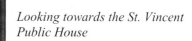

Franke the Hairdressers

Ladywood Community Centre

Inside of the community centre

Youngsters enjoying Saturday afternoon practicing their musical skills

LADYWOOD COMMUNITY PROJECT

DROP - IN
12pm- 3.30pm Monday- Friday.
For parents and children.
Free tea and coffee!
Plenty of toys and good play facilities.
Regular childrens activities.

WOMENS GROUP
Regular shopping trips to low- cost supermarkets.
Local trips out for parents & children.
Various group activities & discussion.
Creche available for most activities.
Your suggested are valued !

DAY TRIPS OUT
To the seaside and popular theme parks.
Usually 3 or 4 a year advertised locally.

WRIGGLERS
Monday 10.30am for people
who have care of a baby or toddler.

ADVICE
Available on a wide range of issues:
debt, fuel, welfare benefits, childcare, and domestic violence.
Referral agency for Ladywood Furniture Project. Social Worker and
Money Advisor available for more specialist advice- by appointment.

BABY BOUNCERS
Stairgates and fireguards available for loan.
Free of charge for anyone living in Ladywood who recieves any state benefit.
(subject to availability).

CREDIT UNION
Ladywood Credit Union has their registered office here.
Cash point open Monday - Friday 9.30am- 12.00pm.
Tuesday, Wednesday & Thursday 11.30am - 4.00pm.
For more details see Credit Union publicity.

BEFRIENDING SERVICE
A practical & emotional support service for survivors
of domestic violence.

KIDS BARGAIN BUYS
Sale of good quality childrens clothes,
equipment and toys. Members can sell or buy.

St. Vincent Street Club

Church in St. Vincent Street

Gilby Road

*The Old Brethren Hall
(marked with an arrow)*

*Mr. Fellows of the
Brethren Hall (Gospel Hall)*

Ladywood Middleway, 1994

The same view, but in 1999

Above - Gilby Road, 1994 and Below in 1999

Ledsam Street

LADYWOOD

BELLIS & MORCOM LTD.

The original home of A.C.E. Bellis & Co. (known as Bellis and Morcom Ltd.)
Ledsam Street Works, Ledsam Street.
Christmas parties were organised for deprived children of the area

Ledsam Street, 1989

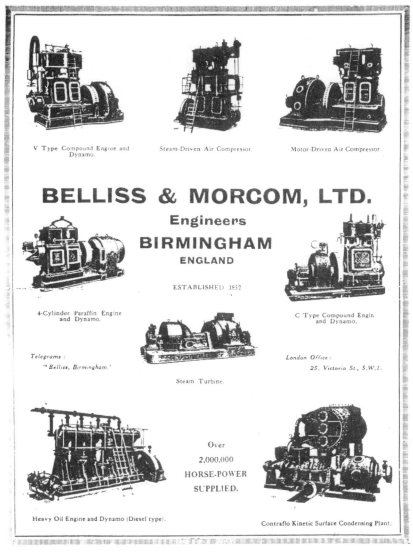

Advert for Bellis & Morcom

Ledsam Street, 1956

*Ladywood House at the junction of Ledsam Street and
St. Vincent Street, known locally as "Mary's"*

The Boys' Brigade marching down Ledsam Street a sight you don't see now

REGENT CINEMA

The new Regent Cinema in Ledsam Street was known as the "Ledsam" to the local residents. Although someone told me that it used to be called the "louse" because you went in without a cardigan and came out with a knitted one!!!

Although this is not a very good reproduction from the original photograph, the films showing on 16th August 1957 are "Shack Out on 101" starring Terry Moore, and was an "A"; the other film is "Tarzan Triumph" and was a "U".

"The Ledsam" was known locally as the "Blood Tub", Saturday afternoon – 1d crush – Tom Mix, Evil Dr. Fu Man Chu; no matter how frightened you were you just had to go next week to see what evil he was up to again!

The place for courting couples was Ledsam Street, known to the locals as "The Monkey Run".

Ladywood Family Centre

The Duchess of Gloucester opening Children Nursery in Ladywood

The Children's Home was on Tuesday, 16 November 1971 by the Duchess of Gloucester. The Centre, which is within half-mile of the city centre undertakes community work of a specialist nature. It is a day care centre for the pre-school groups up of to 20 children.

The project was not simply a day minding exercise, but was aimed at "prevention". This included preventing possible family breakdown and the consequent need for a child to be taken into care; preventing language and intellectual handicaps; developing children who live in culturally deprived homes and, in the case of children with mental and physical disabilities. A compensatory programme was developed to help them overcome their handicaps.

The Centre was not intended to be used only for day care, but also to provide a base and meeting point for social workers serving the Ladywood area and a focal point for child care training and experimental family casework.

The centre had two closely integrated components, one covering extended day care, rather on the pattern of day nurseries; the other a nursery school but aiming to compensate the children for their disabilities.

The cost of the building was £81,7000, the warden at the time of the opening was Mr. W. J. Garbett.

Ruston Street

LADYWOOD

SHOPS AND BUSINESSES - 1933

Fred Fear, 123 Ruston Street - House - cum - Shop. Entry was up 2 steps, and there was a curtain around a counter, where they would be sitting in front of the fire

Elizabeth Ricketts, 124 Ruston Street

Clara Llewellyn, Draper, 117 Ruston Street - This was only a small shop. Clara later moved to America to live.

Eccles, Outdoor

Gabrielles, General Store

Parkes, Sweet Shop

Theatrical Make-up Shop, Sold make-up and jewellery and was situated at the corner of Ruston Street and Broad Street

Florence Georgina Walker, Pawnbroker, 76 Ruston Street - Known as Polly Walkers

A1 Screw Company, 81 Ruston Street - Nut manufacturers

Charles Jackson, Chimney Sweep, 30 Ruston Street

21 Ruston Street

Mr. and Mrs. Fear's shop

Mrs. Fear and her daughter, Nellie are on the step

In front of them is Mrs. Crighton

Mrs. Elsy lived in the house to the left of the shop

The following article appeared in the Birmingham Evening Mail

"BABE IN THE WOOD"

A Birmingham tank trooper of an armoured division has qualified to play the leading role in "Babes in the Wood". He is trooper T. Fear of 123 Ruston Street, Ladywood.

In the fighting in Normandy, he was in his tank when it was blown up by a mine. Trooper Fear was knocked out with the blast of the explosion, and as the division had to press on, he was laid by the side of the road to await the arrival of the medical officer, who was following up and dealing with casualties. Before the M.O. arrived, Trooper Fear revived, and was surprised to find a pleasant perfume in the air, he was covered with flowers. He pinched himself to make sure he was still alive.

It was then he realised that the local French people must have thought him dead, for they had certainly done him proud in the way of floral tributes. However, he was far from dead.

SILVER JUBILEE - 1937

Left to Right at the entry: Tommy Fear, Les Hughes, Nellie Fear, Gwen Fear
In the road: Mr. and Mrs. Hughes. The Austin 7 car belonged to Mr. Fear

Sitting Down: Tom Fear and Ron Hughes
Background: Mrs. Wheeler, Mrs. Russell, Edna Wheeler, Cyril Stevens and Mrs. Vernon

SILVER JUBILEE - 1937

Front: Mr. Harbridge, Mrs. Till from the Outdoor, corner of Morville Street and Ruston Street - Behind: Mrs. Russell, Jessie Gilliver, Mrs. Vernon, Gladys Savage, June Ricketts, Mrs. Smallwood, Alice Cleaver, Nellie Fear, Ron Hughes, Muriel Smallwood, Joyce Hughes, Norman Wheeler, Mr. Gilliver, Ron Hughes, Norah Gilliver and Mrs. Stacey

Geoffrey Lloyd and Dr. Glass (both under the umbrella), Mrs. Meddings, Mr. Shepherd, Mr. Stockton, Mrs. Shepherd - Back row: Tommy Fear (left with the glasses)

This photograph shows a railwayman with his horse after making deliveries to factories in Ruston Street. It became a tradition to feed this horse, and he is seen here being fed by Mrs. Crighton, outside Fear's shop at 123 Ruston Street, Ladywood

1905 Postcard of Charlie and Flo Compton

Another family picture of Charlie and Flo Compton

Hickman's

LADYWOOD

HICKMAN'S - GREENGROCERS

The business started approximately 100 years ago, when Tom Hickman married a lady, who as far as is known, was in the greengrocery business. He had been involved in making pen nibs.

The original shop was believed to be on the Sandpits. The next move was a shop in King Edward's Road on the corner of Alexander Street. Soon after a move was made down the road to a shop on the corner of Nelson Street and King Edward's Road.

Tom's son, Ralph, was next in line. He married Pem Moseley (who had connections with Birmingham's best-known fruit market traders in the Bull Ring - Percy Moseley with his family of daughters).

Their son was Alfred (known as Fred Snr.). He had the shop modernised in the late 1930's (Picture above shows the shop before this happened). His two sisters, Ada (who married another well known greengrocer, Charlie Walker of Acocks Green and May, who married Fred Woodward, not in the greengrocery business.

Fred married Irene Boyd in the early 1920's. He acquired another shop in 1938 in Monument Road - near Icknield Port Road.

Then came the 1939-45 war. Quite a few staff, including Fred Jnr., were called up for Army service. This period is probably the most interesting because like a lot of other businesses, the women had to do most of the work.

Rene ran Monument Road, while Fred ran Nelson Street. Many hundreds of Ladywood people were grateful for fish, rabbits and fresh veg in the wartime shortages, as they were, in the depression of the 1930's when Fred Hickman helped many who were destitute.

Fred Jnr. took more control on his release from the Army and his younger brothers Ralph and Barrie started work in the late 1940's. Another shop in Monument Road was taken over, Tromans, in the early 1950's.

In the early 1970's, redevelopment closed the two bigger shops - St. Vincent Street was the new site. Tromans old shop was then demolished. Shortly after, Fred Jnr. died. Soon after, Fred Snr. also died. Nephew Robert joined Ralph and Barrie.

Another shop at Bearwood was acquired in the mid-1980's and was there until 1990.

The shop in St. Vincent Street

Names of staff from the last few years who have worked for Hickman's: *Harry Roath, Roger Taylor, Stella Plant, Sid Taylor, Albert Fisher, Nell Molloy, Eddie Harrington, Len Harrington, Barry Harrington, Mary West, Ellen Roath, Charlie Wheeler, Gorge Rafferty, Les Hill, Pauline Ashley, Ginny Lee, Sid Holloway, Dolly Freer, Rita ..... , Betty Young, Ivy Young, Zena Parker, Old Jack, Nellie Woodhall, Harold Green, there are many, many other people who worked full and part-time, but all the names are very difficult to recollect.*

Mr. Fred Hickman, Snr., was well known for juggling oranges and eggs on his arm. Joan Scarrett and Irene Smith also worked many hours and days in the shop.

Harry Roath - the voice - has always worked for Hickman's, but he has now retired and lives in Quinton. He earned his nickname from always shouting out the price of the produce.

Harry Roath serving a customer in Hickman's

Margaret Thatcher visit's Hickman's

Margaret Thatcher talks to Rene Hickman
in the shop in Ladywood during a bye-election

Landon's

LADYWOOD

LANDON AND SON

Landon and Son were established in Ladywood long before the redevelopment of the area.

The original beginning was a yard in Steward Street, where Mr. Landon ran a Café serving some 100 meals a day. The picture below shows the café with the Plumbing and Plastering sign above the door. After Steward Street they moved to Spring Hill.

Mr. Landon and his late sister, Mrs. Laura Cooper outside the Steward Street cafe

Later on, premises were purchased in Monument Road, next to Monument Road Baths. Milliners previously used the premises. The Landons sold plumbing equipment and other goods, and one side of the shop sold HATS that were left from the previous owner, this only happened while they had hats to sell!

In 1967 they moved to Freeth Street, then in 1969 to their present accommodation in Icknield Port Road (the Old Crown Picture House). Selling a wide range of Bathroom equipment, plumbing and accessories, they still flourish today.

Front of shop

Shop in Freeth Street

The shop in Monument Road

The present shop in Icknield Port Road (formerly the Crown Cinema)

Entertainment

LADYWOOD

New Palace Theatre on the corner of Icknield Street and Spring Hill. Now showing "The Secret Wedding"

THE CROWN PICTURE HOUSE

The Crown Picture House in Icknield Port Road opened on 26th December 1927 and the architect was Mr. Harold Seymour Scott.

This cinema was a regular Saturday morning haunt for youngsters, especially those in the ABC Minors Club. If you were lucky enough to have a birthday whilst in this club, you were invited on to the stage.

Unfortunately the Crown closed its doors on 14th January 1961 and the last film was "The Angry Red Planet", and the last record was "Rose of England".

The building is still there, unlike the rest of the cinemas in the area, and is now owned by Landon's.

For those interested in dimensions: Cinema - 6546 sq. mts.   Car Park - 845 sq. mts.

Were you a member of the ABC Minors?

Remember those Saturdays when you could go on the stage when it was your birthday?

Remember watching those great films, then coming out and pretending to be the hero of the film whether it was the Cowboy or Indian, Pirate or Flash Gordon?

PUBLIC HOUSES

The Squirrel, Morville Street - Built on the site of the old Eagle and Ball – Licensee Mr. A. J. O'Connell, 1989

The Welcome, Ladywood Middleway – Licensee Mr. D. J. Worrall, 1989

The Pied Piper, Ledsam Street – Licensee M. A. Haylett, 1989

The Bricklayers Arms, Icknield Port Road – Licensee Mr. A. G. A. Freeth, 1989

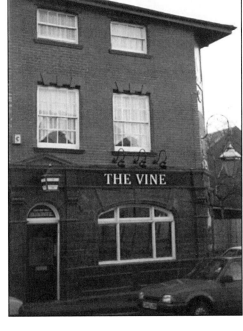

The Vine, Ruston Street – Licensee Mr. R. H. Birch, 1989

St. Vincent, St. Vincent Street – Licensee Mr. R. Haylett, 1989

The City Tavern, Bishopsgate Street – Licensee Mr. C. Bird, 1989

The Shakespeare Inn

The White Swan, Grosvenor Street West – Licensee Kathleen Mary Harnett, 1989

Freeth Arms

*The Belle Vue, Icknield Port Road –
Licensee Rosetta Neale, 1989*

Cross Keys, Steward Street

The Crown, Broad Street

Regulars who have just returned from a charabanc outing - and then posed for this photograph outside the Crown Inn, Broad Street

The Crown, Broad Street –
Licensee Charles Guise with sisters Freda and Dorothy Compton
during a Dinner Dance for the Crown Darts Club, 1953

Edgbaston Reservoir

Families enjoying the Reservoir during the summer

The bandstand in the Reservoir

The Tower Ballroom

The Tower ballroom is situated within the area of Edgbaston Reservoir (the Rezzer) and became a popular meeting place for the old and young, not only of Ladywood, but the whole of Birmingham.

The Tower has been home to dancing, roller-skating and TV series "Boon" was filmed here.

The Tower became a thriving dance hall, and in 1962 the Mecca Organisation obtained the lease, and then renovated the old premises adding luxury and colourful decoration.

Even now the Tower is still a popular dance venue, catering for as many people. Most of the clientele are of the 21's to 40 year's age group who like to dance to live music.

In addition to public dances, they also increased their capacity of banqueting and function business.

Presentation Evening for the Reservoir and District Darts League

Left and right: dancing and drinking at The Tower

A Ladywood family enjoying night out at The Crown, Broad Street

Lloyds Rhythmic Band, who played regularly at the Edgbaston Assembly Rooms, Francis Road.

It cost 3/- entrance fee at the Assembly Rooms and 2/6 at Paradise Street

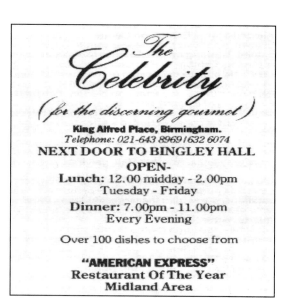

Local people enjoying themselves with the old fashioned accordion and songs

BINGLEY HALL

National Trades Exhibition, this used to last about 8 weeks during the 1920's and the profits were donated to the Hospital Saturday Fund. The highlight of the show used to be at 9 p.m. when they illuminated the "Fairy Fountain", the lights of many colours shone through the spray of the water jets as they shot high into the air, and quickly after, formed a fine mist-like cloud. Children always eagerly awaited this spectacular display.

The Birmingham Post

PRESENTS

The British Theatre Exhibition

BINGLEY HALL
BIRMINGHAM

May 23 to June 18, 1949

The British Theatre Exhibition
was held on June 18 1949

Ideal Home Exhibition

The biggest attraction for Brummies used to be the Ideal Homes Exhibition, did you remember the dancing waters, there was always a house and people still have items purchased at the exhibition.

Where you ever stopped with your Evening Mail and asked for the password?

Did you use to walk around with the Mail under your arm and the password showing, hoping you would be stopped?

What about the Blue Star, did you ever find one?

69

Families enjoying themselves in Wood Street

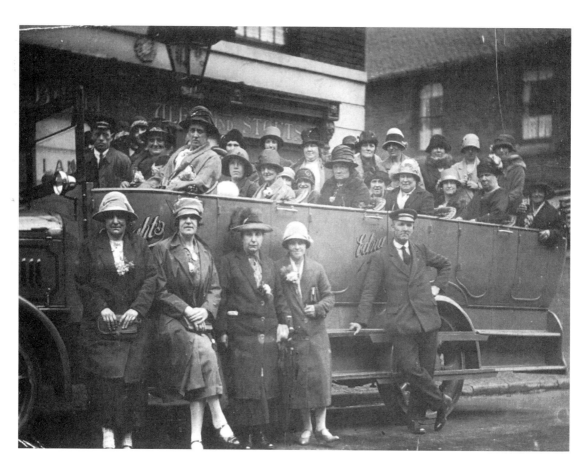

Regulars outside the Rose and Crown set for the annual charabanc outing

Schools

LADYWOOD

The Oratory School, Hyde Road and Oliver Road - Opened in 1856

Steward Street, School, Steward Street - Opened in 1873 - Closed in 1969

Nelson Street School, Nelson Street - Opened in 1876 - Closed in 1939

St. Mark's School, King Edward's Road/St. Mark's Street - Opened in 1843 - Closed in 1940

St. Barnabas School, Ryland Street - Opened in 1862

Birmingham and Edgbaston British School - Opened in 1837 - Closed in 1873

Immanuel School, Tennant Street - Opened in 1872 - Closed in 1937

St. Chad's R.C. School, Summer Hill Terrace - Opened in 1858 - Closed in 1873

Church of the Messiah British School, Broad Street - Opened in 1868 - Closed in 1879

Oozells Street Board School, Oozells Street - Opened in 1878 - Closed in 1906

Edward Street Board School, Edward Street - Opened in 1852 - Closed in 1876

St. Margaret's School, 14a Rann Street

St. Peter's R.C. School, Broad Street - Opened in 1834 - Closed in 1970.

Osler Street Infants, Parents' Day 1928

Osler Street Class IV

Osler Street Boys School Football Team, 1947-48

Osler Street Infants School, Empire Pageant 1929

Osler Street School in the '20s

Osler Street before it was demolished. The Boys school was on the ground floor and the Girls' School on the first floor. Prefects used to stand at the gate and if you were late you were reported to the headteacher.

*Leaving Certificate,
Osler Street Senior Girls, 1937*

Head teacher: J. F. Craig

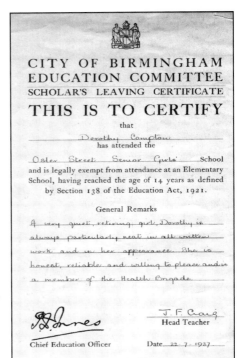

Osler Street Boys' School, 1949

This photograph was taken approximately 60 years ago at Osler Street Infants School. Stan Pearsall is on the front row to the right, other names are Bill leaver, George Scrivens, Arthur Watson, Bill Mustin, Jim Hanson, Fred Clark, Florrie Low, and Elsie Bagnell

Leaving certificate Osler Street Boys, 1963

Headteacher A. W. Upton

St. John's School

*Girls from St. Barnabas School, Ryland Street at camp,
pictured are Florrie Compton, Dora Gumbley, Alice
Copson, Betty Protheroe, Joan Scarrot*

Winnifred Walker, 1931, St. Patrick's School

ST. GEORGE'S SCHOOL

Extracts from an article written by Mr. Pillinger, former Headteacher, St. George's School

At a vestry meeting held at St. George's Church on 25th October 1852, a committee was formed under the Chairmanship of the Rev. E. Lillingston. It styled itself the St. George's District Infants' School Committee and was born from a resolution, which stated that "the increasing population in St. George's district renders it desirable that an Infant School for the use of the poor should be erected in the neighbourhood of Monument Lane. Much of the discussions and planning were done at Mr. Winfield's works in Cambridge Street. His is a name well known to some members of our parish and he was a prime mover in the scheme.

St. George's School around the turn of the century

The Committee eventually settled on a site in Plough and Harrow Road and after canvassing the whole district and as a result of the Vicar's Pastoral Letter and several moving sermons a substantial sum of money was promised. This, with prospective grants made it possible to start on the erection of an Infants' School and a house for the Mistress. This part of our present buildings is the section fronting Plough and Harrow road. Its cost was £900 and the house cost £250. The Government Grant towards this was £182 and the National Society £45. So this missionary act of faith on the part of the Parish in 1852-3-4 cost over £900, and that was only the beginning. By the end of February 1854 the school was ready for use.

This flourishing condition of the school called for the immediate extension of the building; in fact Her Majesty's Inspector reported that "the children were so thick upon the ground that it materially interfered with the necessary discipline of the school". And so the new wing for the school was born, this being the section facing Beaufort Road, the present centre of the school. It was intended to separate the Infants from the older children, but this does not seem to have been accomplished until 1886.

The first Headmaster was Mr. W. J. Arnott, who was trained at St. Paul's College, Cheltenham. His salary was to be £80 for the first year, and £100 for the second, plus a quarter of the Government Grant.

In 1876, for instance, "One dozen shirts were sent to Mrs. Lea (work of the girls in Std. 4 and 5)" and in 1885 "Received parcel for work from Miss Badger (12 brown calico shirts and 12 flannel petticoats from Blind Asylum)". Miss Badger, by the way established the first Blind School in Birmingham in a private house in Ryland Street.

In 1883 the Headmaster of the Boys' School writes: "I have bought a Magic Lantern for the school for £7 intending to use as an educational instrument".

1890 - "The Swimming class excites great interest among the boys of the upper three classes. 43 went this morning".

The Junior School

The Infants School

The following extracts from the logbooks of the school indicate the way in which the children profited from the extended education service:

1920 - February - 50 boys visited Exhibition of Drawings at Society of Artists.

55 boys and two teachers went to Summerfield Park for organised games.

The School Dentist examined teeth of girls of nine and twelve years of age.

30 Boys visited the School for Jewellers in Victoria Street and 30 Boys visited the Central Library and the Child Librarian spoke on "How to use the Reference Library".

1921 - Sidney Harrison has obtained a Scholarship at Aston Commercial School.

1922 - Today I visited the Science Centre in Monument Road and the Metal Work Centre at Osler Street.

1924 - At the invitation of the Managers of the Birmingham Station of the British Broadcasting Company, scenes from "Twelfth Night" were broadcast by the School Dramatic Club this afternoon.

A party of senior boys together with two members of Staff visited the Empire Exhibition at Wembley.

1925 - I visited the Cookery and Laundry Centre in Bath Row and saw our senior girls at work.

In August 1939, all school staff were recalled from their holidays to plan the mass evacuation of those children whose parents wished them to go to safer areas. "Our children were scheduled to go to Lickey End and on 1st September a party of 45, with teachers and helpers made the journey and by mid-day they were safely billeted with their foster parents.

Being so near to Birmingham, the group at Lickey End rapidly dwindled and by January 1940, only 13 of the original 45 remained.

Class of the 1950's with Mr. Wilfred Pillinger, Headmaster.
Also pictured Malcolm Shiner (middle row, second from right)
Malcolm Joseph, Clive Jones (bottom row, last two on the right)

We shall long remember the events of 1954, the Centenary Year of the School. The Centenary Service, when everybody rallied in the sunshine at the school and marched in procession as in years past to the Parish Church; the miracle of that day in June, which turned out to be the hottest day in a very wet and cold summer and when six coaches of happy children and parents went to Weston-Super-Mare; and then the two most enjoyable display days for parents; and finally a special Christmas entertainment and two wonderful parties.

Nelson Street School

St. Mark's School, 1941

Tennant Street School

ST. PATRICK'S SCHOOL

Above: St. Patrick's School 1931

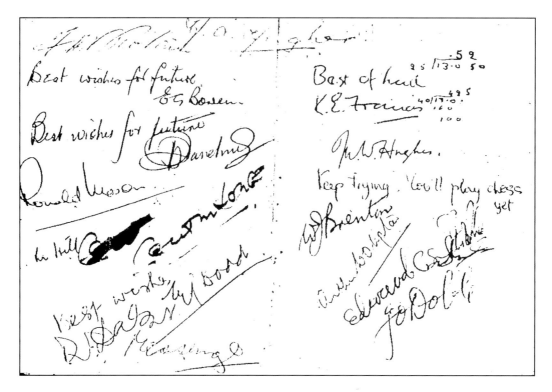

Autographs of teachers from Osler Street Boys' School, 1963

Summerfield Swimming Club

LADYWOOD

SUMMERFIELD SWIMMING CLUB

The Summerfield Swimming Club was set up at Monument Road Baths during 1915. P. Harold Wigley started it in connection with Christ Church, Summerfield.

Harold, as he liked to be called, retired in 1958 after a long and successful time with the swimming club. The club was finally wound up sometime during the 1970's.

Dr. Louis Glass was at one time President and another well-known person Air Vice Marshall Sir Charles Guest was also associated with the club.

Water Polo Team Champions 3rd Division 1928

The club met on Friday evenings for swimming instruction, general swimming and also for competitions and water polo matches against other clubs in the Birmingham and Midland area. After a pleasant evening of swimming and water polo members would often retire to the café opposite the baths, and treat themselves to a cup of tea and perhaps a slice of bread pudding for the princely sum of a 1/2d.

GENTEEL POVERTY-SWIMMING CLUB'S "COMING OF AGE"

MARCH 1936

CLUB'S "COMING-OF-AGE"

No little of the success of the Summerfield Swimming Club, Birmingham, is due to the fact that, throughout the 21 years of its existence, it has been able to retain one man in a secretarial capacity.

The club is celebrating its coming-of-age with a supper dance at the Farcroft Hotel, Handsworth, on Monday next, and the presidents of the leading swimming associations in the Midlands will be present.

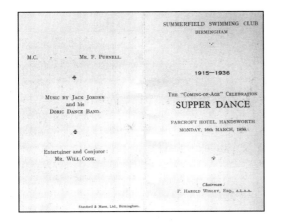 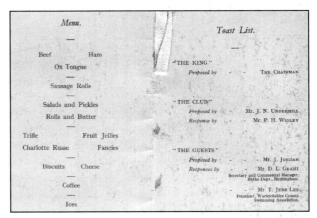

Menu for the "Coming of Age" Supper Dance

Mr. P. H. Wigley was elected secretary at the age of 16. During two years, when he was studying for an accountant's examination, he relinquished the chief post, but rendered help as the assistant scribe of the club. After passing his examination he resumed full responsibility.

It is, therefore, fitting that he should be president of the club for the coming-of-age year.

Mr. Wigley is in the office of the Birmingham Tramways Department, where he has as colleagues, Mr. W. Turner, immediate past president of the Amateur Swimming Association (Midland District), and Mr. P. A. (Nap) Atkin, who has been aptly described as the "Peter Pan" of the swimming world.

First called the Christ Church, Summerfield Swimming Club, the club started in difficult times -1915, and later, owing to many of the officials and members serving with the forces abroad, its activities were for a time suspended. The peak year for membership was 1925, when the active roll had 197 names. The club has met at Monument Road, and hopes to expand when the new baths are erected there.

Members of the swimming club already to take the plunge in the Annual Mile Race 1930 at Powells Pool, Sutton Coldfield

Each year the club held a mile swim. Over the years it took place at various venues including-Stratford-on-Avon, Powells Pool in Sutton Park, Twyning Fleet near Tewkesbury and Upton-upon-Severn. It was a very enjoyable family occasion. Members together with family and friends would travel to the appointed place by coach and cars. The mile race usually started about mid-day. Half of the race was against the current and half of it with the current. After the race members would have a picnic style lunch and a free afternoon to do as they wished. At a pre-arranged time groups met up again to go for a High Tea in a local restaurant or function room. A few short speeches and distribution of awards for the mile swim competitors followed the tea. On conclusion of proceedings the coach and cars would depart for home, often calling in at a suitable hostelry for a few drinks to finish off what had been a most enjoyable day out.

Another big occasion was the annual gala, which was held at the Woodcock Street baths in the centre of Birmingham. As well as the club swimming and diving championships there were novelty races and various swimming demonstrations. The evening would usually finish with a friendly water polo match. Afterwards the competitors, along with their families and friends, would gather in the clubroom for refreshments provided by some of the membership.

Memories

LADYWOOD

Memories of Dorothy Leaver – nee Compton

I was born in Morville Street, Ladywood in 1923, I am now 74 years old and would not have changed my childhood for anything, and in those days there was a lovely atmosphere, always love and affection.

Our yard, 1/57 Morville Street, was opposite the Methodist Chapel, towards the Eagle and Ball pub. The neighbours were like one big happy family, my dad was a butcher at Wards in Broad Street for over 50 years, also his two brothers, Fred and Charlie, they were ham and bacon curers; next door neighbours were Mr. Harbridge a milkman; then Mr. Peace, a postman; Mr. Rodis, a railwayman.

Every May Day Mr. Roddis would give Freda and myself a ride on the horse and cart, as they were all trimmed up in those days. The houses were so small, but immaculate, the entries were swilled down, even round the dustbins or should I say Miskins!

The Chapel holds some of my loveliest memories. On anniversaries a very small organ was bought out into the street and a Mr. Darlington conducted the singing, what a lovely fatherly man, everybody loved him.

There was also another organ in the chapel which had bellows pumped by a man called Ernie, to start it. Mr. and Mrs. Meek were the caretakers then and there were steps, steep ones at the side of the Chapel where the coal was kept.

One sad memory was that of a horse which bolted down Ruston Street and went straight into the window of Mr. and Mrs. Knight's, I'll never forget it, the horse had to be shot, but fortunately no-one was injured.

Dorothy Compton
with the accordion

My parents were George and Edith Compton, and although money was scarce in those days we were never short of food, Christmas was lovely they gave us all they could. I remember I longed for an accordion, and they bought me one from the Co-Op in High Street it was £3 10s 0d, a lot of money in those days. I was 11 years old at the time, that same accordion has been my life, and I am still playing it now.

When the lads came home from the war, they always called for me to play at the parties, no modern keyboards like now, my sister Freda used to go with me everytime – we were always together.

The day that they declared that war was over I was playing the accordion outside the Crown Pub in Broad Street and that is were I met my husband, Bill Leaver. He proposed to me after 2 years on the top of the Number 33 Ladywood tram.

The shops in Morville Street were friendly, even if they were small. At Bennett's we were able to buy a sugar pig for 1/2d; Millies with the cigarette machine outside on the wall 2d for 5 woodbines or club cigarettes. If you saved the coupons you could get fruit dishes, even a pair of shoes; I still have a willow pattern fruit dish from Mother's Sunlight Soap coupons.

Rose's shop on the corner of Morville Street/Ruston Street always had a large shoulder of bacon hung in muslin hanging from the ceiling; Fears shop - a house in one – a green curtain hung on a brass rod to divide their living quarters and Tommy, their son, would be playing the piano. Then Stockton's who sold newspapers and comics; Sollors next door to Value House, they were noted for 1/2d pie and ice creams!

Till's the outdoor, if you fetched a pint of beer in a bottle under the age of 14, a label was put on the cork. Cox's, fish and chip shop, next to Millie's. Mrs. Cox would walk to the fish market at 6 a.m. pushing a wicker carriage – it had 3 wheels – to fetch the lovely fish from the market, nothing frozen then! If we took our newspapers to her she would always give us the crispy bits left from the batter!

It was hard work in those days, outside taps, toilets down the yard, brewhouse, and sometimes I wonder how we survived, but we did.

First Prize Certificate presented to Dolly Leaver (nee Compton) from Morville Street Methodist Church, 1936

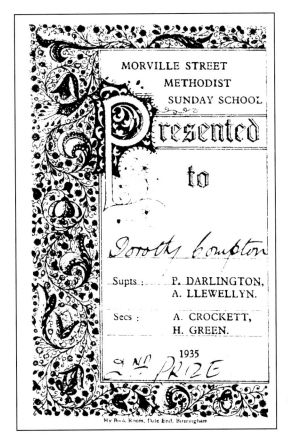

Second Prize Certificate presented to Dolly Leaver (nee Compton) from Morville Street Methodist Church, 1935

"KEEPING THE HOME FIRES BURNING"

Keeping our homes warm today is a fairly simple matter. We only have to flick a switch and on comes the central heating or electric fire. At the turn of a knob on comes the gas fire. What a difference it was years ago when most homes had an old black lead grate with an open coal fire. Old newspaper had to be laid in the fire basket, followed by some pieces of firewood, they were then covered with small pieces of coal and then the paper was lit with a match. If you had some "bad" coal or if the wind was a little strong in the chimney then a metal "draw-tin" was placed over the fire basket to help the fire to catch. The following morning all the cold dead ashes had to be removed so that you could start all over again.

During the war years, especially when coal was rationed, many an ingenious way of providing heat was used. As a lad I can remember going down to Wheelers greengrocery shop in Ryland Street with my home made "box on wheels" cart to get some logs which he used to have occasionally. These used to supplement the coal ration. By getting a glowing bed of hot coal and then putting a log in the centre, it would then last us the rest of the day. Another thing was making good use of the slack in the coal. My mother used to get a bucket of slack and add some ordinary flour, then add some water and mix the lot up into a stiff paste. We then took handfuls and shaped them into round nuggets and left then to dry hard. They burned beautifully with no waste.

Mr. Riley, the coal merchant, used to sell coal direct from the coal wharf, which was at the bottom of Morville Street and Browning Street. The coal was brought to the wharf by canal barge, which ran at the back of the wharf.

My mother tells me that Mr. Riley was very strict about distribution of the rationed coal. People would queue at the wharf with all manner of transport to carry the coal away with. Some would carry sacks, others would have barrows, prams, pushchairs, anything on wheels. Mr. Riley used to allow each person ¼ cwt, for which he used to charge 4½d. He would say that at least everyone had some coal for a fire. He also delivered coal around the area.

The back to back houses up the yards that we used to live in didn't have any cellars like the houses on the streets. Our "coal-holes" were under the stairs and when the coalman arrived my mother would open the door of the "coal-hole" and open the house door. She would then lay sheets of newspaper down on the floor making a path across the living room and into the kitchen area where the stairs were. The coalman would then carry a bag of coal on his back up the yard and then into the house and empty it into the pace under the stairs, coal dust everywhere. We would have five or six bags at a time and my job was to keep count of the number of bags, just to make sure.

Yes, heating is something we take for granted today.

Phil Trentham

MEMORIES OF LADYWOOD

SCOUTS - At the end of the first evening at scouts, I came down the stairs into the yard, and saw a brand new racing bike with fixed wheel. One of the older scouts asked if I wanted a ride on it. After a few yards, the scoutmaster shouted "where are you going on my bike", I raced up the road, then put the bike up against a lamp-post, and ran down the nearest entry, through someone's garden, over the wall and never to be seen again.

CRICKET - Vicar Darrell of St. John's, Monument Road, had a son Jeff, who was the local heartthrob. He played cricket on a large lawn, at the side of the vicarage. My sister was watching him play one day, when Jeff hit the ball high into the air. She was too busy watching Jeff, and wasn't aware that the ball was about to hit her on the head. When she opened her eyes, Jeff Darrell asked is if she was all right, that was worth all the pain!

AIR RAID SHELTER - My father was an air-raid warden. A bomb hit the Borax Works, next to Bellis and Morcom, Dad put a hat on me and took me outside, and the sky was all the colours of a rainbow.

CO-OP HORSE - One Saturday morning I was playing in the yard, 1/57 Morville Street, suddenly a terrible crash was heard. It was the "Co-Op bread horse" which had been frightened by a car horn. The horse bolted and crashed into Mrs. Knight's front house in Morville Street, opposite Ruston Street.

NEIGHBOURS - All the neighbours in our yard were working. My father, George Compton, butcher; Mr. Harbridge, milkman; Mr. Peace, postman; Mr. Roddis, railwayman. Every 1st May, Mr. Roddis would bring his horse round, it was all trimmed up and he gave us a ride.

ANNIVERSARY SUNDAY'S - A miniature organ was taken into the street, where we all sang hymns with the committee, Mr. Darlington, Mr. Green and Mr. Llewellyn. They also had their own cricket team. Weddings also took place there. I went to Christian Endeavour once a week.

ST. MARGARET'S - St. Margaret's Church in Ledsam Street, used to have a procession around the streets of Ladywood every Sunday. They always, as they paraded, used to swing incense in canisters (horrible smell).

JOE WILLIAMS - Mr. Williams was a milkman. He came round selling milk direct from a churn for 11/2d. a pint.

HANGERS - This received a direct bomb hit during the war and two of my friends were killed, Stanley Capewell and Denis Savage.

Memories of Mrs. Hurst

I was born in Bishopsgate Street and life revolved around Emmanuel Church and school. My parents owned a small shop selling mostly groceries, sweets and tobacco. The shop next door was "Reynolds" a toy shop, also selling oddments, mops and buckets etc. These shops backed onto Tennant Street.

Mrs. Gertrude Hurst and her sister, Gladys, outside the shop

Mrs. Beddowes (Mrs. Hurst's mother)

We shopped in Broad Street and also went to church there. My father joined the club in Broad Street (Working Men's). Sad to say he only did 3 days work each week at a sheet metal factory in Aston. My mother worked very hard in the shop from 7 until 8 at night, Sunday all day off. The photo shows the Pawn Shop, Barbers and a shop we called Sammy Salt, it was filled with cats and all sorts, today it would not be allowed. Finally when he died the corporation sorted it out. We had to close the shop doors because it was so smelly. It changed into a clothes shop.

My special friend, Ethel, lived close by and we all appeared happy. I did long for a garden and bathroom. My friend lived in a small front house they had to go quite a way to the lavatory and wash house, lucky for us we had our own. My uncle and aunt had a baker's shop and the bakehouse was in the yard. Of course this would not be allowed today. After leaving Emmanuel School, I went to Piggot Street School opposite the Queen's Hospital.

My Granny lived in Grant Street. I believe that was in the Edgbaston area. Broad Street was good shopping, Sibley's was a high-class clothes shop and we went there on special occasions, we also had photographs taken at Wynnes.

Ledsam Street was near our shop and we used to go to the Lyric Cinema there. I went to see Charlie Chaplin at the Lyric. Summerhill Street brings back memories, my auntie at the bakers moved to another shop there. I think it was a fruit shop opposite Nelson Street called Fields, but I'm not to sure. My sister had a friend who lived in a fruit shop in Ledsam Street named Edna Wheeler and they used to meet to go to work at Cadbury's. When I think of young girls like them starting out at 7 a.m. to catch the train from Islington Row, it makes me shiver, just 14 years old.

I eventually worked at Cadbury's myself. Happy days working there, I'm still in touch with what was then called "Cadbury's Angels".

I well remember going with my friends with a wheelbarrow to fetch the coal from Wheeler Lane Wharf, for their mothers. Some were left without fathers, who had died prematurely from TB. The kiddies were well behaved, some passed for the Grammar School, but unable to go for the lack of money.

Going down Tennant Street I remember the place where pigs were killed. It was smelly and running with water.

We looked forward to summer when we could go to "Albrights Field". It was open for the children and Miss Albright was so kind. It was situated in Frederick Road. We had good times playing in the marquee and watching the trains. The old man used to give us drinks of water in heavy iron cups.

My sister, Gladys, is 3rd left (with glasses) on second row.

Most of the children came from Tennant Street, Bishopsgate Street and some from William Street and Granville Street

We did venture to Monument Road to a small park and I got friendly with a girl from Monument Road. They lived at the school there, St. John's I think. Another favourite place was the Botanical Gardens. I loved going to the Reservoir with my Mom, hand in hand, and it reminded me of the seaside.

I don't remember many big families. My sister and I had a happy life just the two of us. My husband came from a big family of 10. The family lived in Hurst Street. Incidentally his name is Fred Hurst, and he left to join up at 18 years of age and joined the Black Watch. Went abroad in 1936. A neighbour of ours in Bishopsgate Street (the toyshop) knew him from working at a factory and he asked me to write Fred in Palestine. I did write but he never had leave because the war came. I was still at Cadbury's. After writing for 8 years, the war was over and he was due home from POW camp in Germany in 1945.

We had never met before and 2 weeks later we married at St. Paul's Church, Balsall Heath. He had been promoted to Staff Sergeant. Our early-married life, with our young son Graham, was spent managing an outward-bound camp in Streetly, for underprivileged Birmingham kids. We then were school caretakers on the Lickey Hills until retirement in 1980 - Thank God we survived, we enjoy life and drive around the country.

Memories of Phil Trentham

This picture of the coach outing was taken outside the Rose Public House, which stood on the corner of Sherbourne Street and St. Vincent Street, Ladywood. It was taken around 1930, and the lady in the middle of the picture on the back row, with the tall black hat on, was my Grandmother, Mrs Rosa Hall and she lived at 17 Morville Street, which was the third house down from the Old Stream Clock pub.

Her husband, Henry Hall, who was also my grandfather, is the person on the left of the picture of the group of men standing outside the Old Steam Clock, smoking his pipe.

My mother can date the picture to the exact day, 10 May 1935; the buntings over the door were to celebrate the Jubilee of King George and Queen Mary.

The Old Steam Clock was my grandfathers local which I used to nip in on occasions as a lad to hand a late bet to him, which he would then have to hurry off and take to the bookies and put it on. He was a grand old chap; he would take my brother and me to the "Ledsam" picture house when we were children once every week in the same seats in the 10d's.

Outside the Old Steam Clock, Morville Street

Now we come forward in time to 1951. The picture is of the 8th Birmingham Company of the Boys Brigade, which was the oldest company in Birmingham. Our headquarters was the chapel on the corner of St. Martin's Street and Tennant Street. I played the side drum in the band that's me in the centre of the drummers.

Boys Brigade marching down Ledsam Street

I was fifteen at the time, and we were parading down Ledsam Street, showing Pearks Stores, which was opposite Friston Street. We were leading the Sunday school procession of children in the background who were from the Morville Street Methodist Chapel. The banner they are carrying says " Morville Street Sunday School Anniversary Today".

Ladywood Chapel

The names of the seven girls on the top row were, reading from left to right: Irene Salter, Elsie Fleet, Pat Dutton, Eana Maddox, Beryl Watts, Rosa Scott and Rita Smith.

From there I courted Rita for six years, during which time I did 2 years national service in Berlin. We were married on the 14 September 1957. Writing these memories has certainly rolled back the years.

Memories of Rose-Marie Orme

I lived at this time in Acocks Green but I had an Aunt, Dorothy (Dolly) Hopkins, who kept a greengrocers shop in Clark Street, Ladywood, it would be around the late 1930's into the 1940's, the shop was just up on the left hand side.

I would come out of school on a Friday afternoon, get a No. 44 bus, then the No.8 Inner Circle to get to the shop so I could help her and stay the weekend with her. I can't remember if the shop's name was Hopkin's or White's. It was great fun being there, we had to go up the entry at the side of the shop into the yard at the back to use the toilets!

I had another aunt, Alice Price, who had a second hand clothes shop in Icknield Port Road, almost opposite Clark Street. I would go to help her sometimes, but I didn't enjoy that as much as the greengrocery.

I can also remember going with my grandmother to visit one of her sisters, again in the mid 1930's to the Almshouses on the corner of Hagley Road and Ladywood Road by the Children's Hospital, these I believe were for ladies only.

Pettit Family – Ryland Street

Pettit's second-hand shop was on the corner of Ryland Street opposite what is now Ryland Garage.

The shop front faced the street, and there was a workshop at the rear. The family lived upstairs.

Mr. Pettit used to hire out handcarts for people moving house, no vans in those days, at 1s. 0d. each, he had about 8-10 carts. Unfortunately some people never returned the carts and left them all over the place, it was a regular occurrence for the police from Summerfield to return a cart to Mr. Pettit.

He also used to buy wood and make props to sell in the shop. If he ever had large pictures for sale, a Mr. Haynes used to buy them from him and sell them from his shop in Broad Street.

Mr. Pettit used to socialise in The Mitre in Ledsam Street, and the shop closed down in the 50's. The shop front was knocked down and altered back into a house. The shop front became the front room and only used on Sundays!

Dennis Pettit

Dennis and a neighbour

To

Edward Pettit has been in my employ about 14 years during which time he has always given me every satisfaction. I believe him to be thoroughly honest & trustworthy & would not doubt acquit himself Creditably in any capacity in which he may be suitably employed.

W. F. Needham

This is a reference for Edward Pettit from W. F.Needham in 1904

Ashforth family – Clissold Street

*Mr. and Mrs. Ashforth
centre and right*

Triplets Vernon, Lewis and John

The Hunt Family - Osler Street

Albert Hunt

Mrs. Hunt outside 41 Osler Street

*Albert's Mother,
on the   right*

*Alberts' Father,
on the left*

David, Jean and Derek Hunt

Derek Hunt

The Hunt family with friends and nieghbours in Osler Street on Coronation Day

Ingleby Street/Eyre Street

*Winnifred Walker, Cyril Huckfield
and a friend*

Winnifred Walker

Mrs. Batt and Mr. Jones

*William Walker and
Louisa Batt*

Lillian Walker and Arthur Kelly

Edith and John Batt

Ingleby Street/Eyre Street

*Winnifred and Lilian
Walker
with Irene Batt*

*Winnifred and Lilian Walker
with Irene Batt*

*William and Nick Walker with
a friend*

Edith Batt and Maud Grinnel

Edith and John Batt

Around the area

LADYWOOD

BEECH STREET

BEECH STREET - This photograph was taken at random, on the 9th November 1965. The two ladies featured, are in fact, my mother, Freda Joseph and grandmother, Edith Compton (who lived in Beech Street). The picture below shows Malcolm Joseph in the garden at Beech Street, and the other is the inside of my grandmother's house.

PERROT'S FOLLY

John Perrot built the monument in 1758. The original land had once belonged to the Lord of the Manor of Birmingham.

This monument has now become known as Perrot's Folly. Mr. Perrot lived in Belbroughton and supposedly had the tower erected so that he could view his property in Belbroughton. Unfortunately the height of land at Clent prevented this, thus the name "Folly".

It is situated on the Rotton Park Estate which John Perrot inherited in 1737, and stands 96ft. high

The monument can now be found in Waterworks Road, and is the home of Meteorological Society of Birmingham.

On 5th August, 1958 an appeal was made for its repair in The Times newspaper, and it is now scheduled as an Ancient Monument

DAVENPORTS

The first record of Davenports as a Midland Brewery was in 1829, when Robert Davenport had premises in Brearley Street, Hockley.

The family run brewery expanded and developed until in 1852 it moved to Bath Row. The business was completely centralised to Bath Row in 1868.

In 1904 the great change came when Baron John Davenport set up the Beer at Home delivery service, which survived two world wars, and established depots throughout the country.

Beer at Home was sold to Hazeldown Supplies in 1985 and it is still selling Davenports. As a result of the introduction of bottled beers, certain casks were set aside for bottling, from this came "Davenports C. B. Ltd.". The original title of "John Davenport and Sons Brewery Ltd." was retained for the retail operation. These ran as separate companies until October 1974, when they were amalgamated to become Davenports Brewery PLC. Davenports pioneered and produced PET bottles and until the recent transfer of operations to Greenalls, bottled and canned beers for outside contracting breweries. Then in 1983, Davenports successfully fought off a take-over bid by Wolverhampton and Dudley Breweries.

1986 saw Davenports integrated into the Greenall Whitley Group, who are based in Warrington, Cheshire. As part of the Group they now have links with the De Vere Hotel Group, Shipstones Brewery in Nottingham, Symonds Cider, Cambrian Soft Drinks, as well as business, catering houses, hotels in Britain and America, Leisure Clubs, Off-licences and bars.

The building in Bath Row, unfortunately it is no longer Davenports

Davenports and the Shrewsbury and Wem Brewery, also part of the Greenall Whitley Group, merged in 1986 and the management functions were concentrated in Birmingham. 1988 saw the closure of the Wem Brewery, and production and transport transferred to Birmingham. The Birmingham site serviced over 260 tenancies, and 64 managed houses trading under Davenports and Wem names under one management, as well as free trade accounts. The Birmingham site employed a total of 130 administrative and sales staff, and over 100 brewery workers, warehousemen and drivers.

Both Davenports and Wem are well known for "award winning beers". Just for example, Davenports won the Sunday Mirror Award in 1978, The International Brewers Exhibition Award twice and the Supreme Champion twice. Wem Bitter was also a winner of the Supreme Champion. Davenports and Wem have produced award-winning beers since the 19th Century and this tradition continues.

Beers and lagers produced in Birmingham, the excellent products produced by our associated companies in the Group together with the recent introduction of Labatts Canadian Lager, marketing expertise and first class licensees, result in a formidable retailing operation.

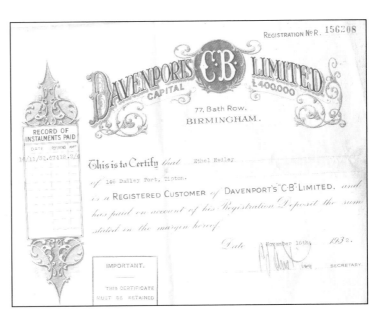

Registered Customer of davenports Certificates Number 156208 in the name of Ethel Hadley, 146 Dudley Port, Tipton

107

THE LADYWOOD LOG

This was a community newspaper which was published during the late 1960's early 1970's for the Ladywood area and has proved to be a difficult item to find out about.

There are no copies or records in the Reference Library, I acquired this copy from a relative who lived in the area.

Ladywood Community Centre News

On Tuesday, 9 June at the inaugural meeting of the Ladywood Ladies Club at the Ladywood Community Centre, Mrs. Cook was elected as the first Chairman, Miss cook as Secretary and Mrs. Holland as Treasurer. The remaining nine members agreed to form the Club's Organising Committee.

This Club is open to all ladies in the area, and the programme will be organised with this in mind; speakers, film shows, beetle drives, social events and outings will be arranged according to the needs and wishes of the members. Tuesday evenings at 7.30 p.m. in Ladywood Community Centre should be worth looking forward to, ladies. Make the old man baby-sit for once and you come along and have good night out every week!

N.C.

Congratulations on the engagement of Miss Susan Hoccom to Mr. Dennis Bull

Any advertisements news items, letters for publication or enquiries should be posted to our Editors:

Miss M. Allwood, 14 Kenchester House, Shylton's Croft, 16
Miss H. Walker, 5 Avery House, Chamberlain Gardens, 16
Mr. R. Cooper, 266 Monument Road, 16

Items from the newspaper

ST. JOHN'S CHURCH

Walking or driving along Ladywood Middleway today a vast housing estate and maisonettes will meet you, compared to years ago when you had shops.

At the top of the Middleway you find a large roundabout and then St. John's Church, it is now surrounded by roads, a satellite amongst businesses and dwarfed beneath Wells Tower.

The first recorded note of St. John's was in 1854, when it was sandwiched between Monument Road (the old Inner Ring Road) and Alston Street.

It was on 17th February 1851, that Mr. Henry Rotten held a meeting at his house to discuss the building of a church to meet the growing spiritual need of the area. The Rev. G. Lea, intimated that he would donate £1,000. The Governors of the King Edward schools had also agreed to allow a site on their property, and the Rector of St. Martin's bestowed an amount of glebe land. It was therefore decided that 1400 placeholders would be built and called the Church of St. John the Evangelist.

The most well known vicar of St. John's was the Rev. Norman Power.

ST. BARNABAS' CHURCH

The Church was erected in 1857 in Ryland Street North, thanks to the generosity of Miss Louisa A. Ryland.

The land and £3,000 were donated by Miss Ryland.

The Foundation stone was laid in 1857.

The Church was consecrated on 24th October, 1860.

Mr. Bourne of Dudley designed the Church and it was based on a parallelogram in plan "Giving a large open timber roof spanning the entire width, with galleries on three sides". The tower was at the north-west angle of the building and was surmounted by an octagonal turret.

My parents were married here and I was christened at St. Barnabas'.

Interior of St. Barnabas' Church

AUGUST 1948

ST. BARNABAS' CHURCH

RYLAND STREET

BIRMINGHAM

PARISH MAGAZINE

∽∽∽∽∽∽∽∽∽

Vicar : Rev. ALFRED T. L. DOYLE, M.A.
66 Beaufort Road, Edgbaston (Tel. : Edg. 2809).

Churchwardens : Messrs. W. Evans and C. Fox.

Lady Worker : Miss F. Gomersal, 76 Beaufort Road.

Verger : Mr. W. Lucock, 67, Ryland Street, to whom notice of Banns of Marriage, Baptisms and Churchings should be given.

Sunday Services : Holy Communion, 8 a.m. (2nd Sunday, 9.30 a.m.), 11 a.m., 1st Sunday ; 6.30 p.m., 2nd and 4th Sundays. Matins, 11 a.m. ; Evensong, 6.30 p.m.

Weekdays : Holy Communion on Festivals and Saints' Days as announced.

Holy Baptism : 2nd and 4th Sundays at 4 p.m.

Bible Class and Sunday Schools : 2.45 p.m. and 3 p.m.

ORGANIZATIONS :

Women's Fellowship, Monday, 3 p.m.
Brownies, Tuesday, 6 p.m.
Scouts, Monday 7 p.m.
Badminton Club, Tuesday, 6.45 p.m.

Girl Guides, Thursday, 7 p.m.
Mothers' Union, 1st Monday in month, 3 p.m.
Cubs, Monday, 5.30 p.m.
Youth Fellowship, Friday, 7.30 p.m.

Mr. A. E. Newnham - After a long period of service, 23 years, in our Junior Schools, Mr. Newnham, our Headmaster has reached the mature age of 65 – the age of retirement. We wish him every blessing in his retirement, which we trust will be long and happy - 1948

Congregational Outing – Saturday, 11th September, leaving the Church at 10 a.m. to Ludlow and Church Stretton, passing Bewdley, Clee Hills, Much Wenlock and Bridgenorth. There are a few seats available in the coach, price 11s. Would those who would like to join the party, please let Miss Gomersal have their names as soon as possible - 1948

St. Barnabas' Parish Magazine

IN MEMORIAM.
MR. FRANCIS HENRY POWELL.

Mr. Powell passed away on July 17, at the age of 85, and thus was removed from our midst a most lovable and kindly character. With his stolid regularity at Church whenever his health allowed, and with his cheerful manner and unassuming Christian helpfulness and old-world courtesy he represented a type of Englishman which this present-day world sorely needs and can ill-afford to lose. We extend our deepest sympathy to all his relatives and friends in their bereavement. The funeral service was held at St. Barnabas, on Thursday, July 22.

VESTRY NOTES.

HOLY BAPTISM.

June 7. Edith Kate Lowe (adult).
,, ,, Anthony Harry Taylor, Jennifer Anne Lane, Michael John Turner, Valerie Joyce Robinson, Janet Downes, John Frank Griffiths.

HOLY MATRIMONY.

June 26. William Henry Leaver to Dorothy May Compton.
July 10. Leslie Norman Lawford to Elsie Leslie.

BURIAL SERVICE.

July 22. Francis Henry Powell, aged 85 years.

ALTAR FLOWERS.

Aug. 8, Mrs. Moore. Aug. 15, Miss M. Way and Miss Thompson. Aug. 22, Mrs. Lucock. Aug. 29, Miss L. Darwood. Sept. 5, Mrs. A. Fox.

SPRING HILL LIBRARY

The Library opened on 7th January 1893. The Birmingham Architects, Martin and Chamberlain designed it. Built 9 years after the death of John Chamberlain, Spring Hill Library shows the continuing influence on the firm of his capacity for bold three-dimensional planning.

Built on the corner of Spring Hill and Icknield Street, the site is a small one for the accommodation required. It is very compact, tall and steep in appearance. Constructed of red brick with a lot of terra cotta, with a red tiled roof.

The tower is 65ft. high, with its four large clockfaces, is a landmark from all directions. The square tower has a hexagonal section with miniature versions of itself on all four corners.

Spring Hill Library made the news when the librarian was attacked with a knife.

In its first year of opening, it issued more books per day than any other branch library.

During the redevelopment of the area, buildings both sides of the library were demolished, and now it stands alone in all its splendour, amongst the modern shops, and need we say graffiti.

In 1968 the library became a listed building, which guarantees that it cannot be demolished out of hand, and if an application were made, there would surely be strong objections.

It was suggested in 1973, that the possibility of moving it en-bloc to another site in Ladywood.

BUSINESSES

Ryland Garage was originally on the corner of Ryland Street and Morville Street until a fire in 1983, which destroyed 75% of the building and all the company records.

The fire-damaged area was recommissioned and premises further up Ryland Street (the old Birmingham Guild buildings) were purchased, and so they are still part of the area.

The original premises formed part of the canal warehouse and there is still evidence of this, and what was the feeder canal was located and filled by the City Council in about 1984-85.

Malcolm James

ENGINEERING

*The gentleman on the right is
Mr. Bullock*

BRUMMAGEM BOATS

Brummagem Boats started at Gas Street Basin with one boat called Brummagem Fly, because "Fly" referred to a cargo type of narrow boat. It carried trippers between Birmingham and Wolverhampton at 12 miles per hour.

In 1976 Gas Street Basin was not large enough to operate from, so they moved to new premises, unfortunately they have now closed down. Sherborne Wharf Heritage Narrow Boats now operate from the site.

The "Brummagem Fly"

"Euphrates Packet"

Newspaper Headlines

Vandals hit church twice

Distraught worshippers were dealt a cruel blow yesterday after their church was ransacked for the second time in six days.

On Sunday thieves made off with collection money and a safe containing documents from the Unitarian church in Ryland Street, Ladywood.

Yesterday vandals again forced their way in and desecrated statutes and furniture.

Last night church official Mrs. Joan Lamb made an urgent appeal to the thieves to return the documents.

"There were marriage and baptism certificates in that safe which are irreplaceable to us and useless to them.

"Even if the thieves dump them somewhere and let us know that would be enough.

"We are all completely shocked by these callous acts. It was bad enough the first time and we had only just got round to clearing up from that incident, but the damage this time is even worse. They've wrecked the place."

Extract from Birmingham Evening Mail
October 1989

Ladywood's sweeping changes

Ladywood residents and school pupils set to work to make their community a better place to live in as part of a campaign to show the council they are environment-friendly.

Squads of cleaners tidied the streets and surrounding areas of Ladywood, St. John's and Nelson secondary schools as well as the Oratory and St. George's Primary Schools between 9.30 a.m. and 12 p.m.

They were responding to Ladywood Community Forum's call to set standards which environmental services should follow.

Extract from Birmingham Evening Mail
1989

Hot stuff from the foundry man!

Shiftwork . . . it's feminine frills from the foundreyman.

Because Laura Shuckburgh's luxury lingerie comes from the firm that former foundry manager Bill Clarke founded.

Bill was made redundant by the company where he had worked for 25 years.

So he set up Clarke Enterprises (Midlands) Ltd. with his daughter, Diane Richards.

Now, instead of steel, it's lingerie that is underpinning his success in shops and mail order business at home, and exports to Sweden and America.

Extract from Birmingham Evening Mail

Bundy Clock

The last tram from Ladywood, 1947

The tram terminus at Icknield Port Road 1947

Above: Little St. Mark's, 1945
Right: Ladywood Chapel
Below Ladywood Unity, 1911

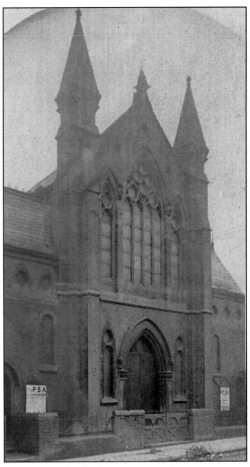

Spring Hill, 1969

Summerhill Road, 1967

The Parade, 1969

The Sandpits

Freeth Street

A small passageway off Cambridge Street

Broad Street looking towards Five Ways

Ryland Street

St. Mark's Street

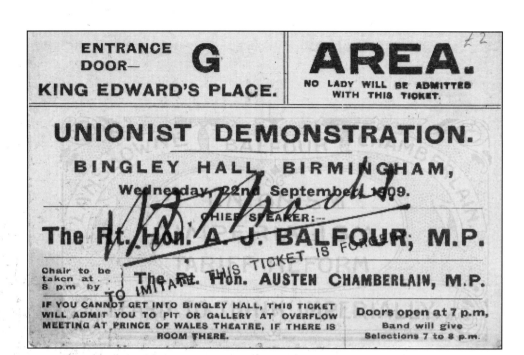

ENTRANCE DOOR— **G** | **AREA.**
KING EDWARD'S PLACE. | NO LADY WILL BE ADMITTED WITH THIS TICKET.

UNIONIST DEMONSTRATION.

BINGLEY HALL, BIRMINGHAM,

Wednesday, 22nd September 1909.

CHIEF SPEAKER:—

The Rt. Hon. A. J. BALFOUR, M.P.

Chair to be taken at 8 p.m. by . . . The Rt. Hon. AUSTEN CHAMBERLAIN, M.P.

IF YOU CANNOT GET INTO BINGLEY HALL, THIS TICKET WILL ADMIT YOU TO PIT OR GALLERY AT OVERFLOW MEETING AT PRINCE OF WALES THEATRE, IF THERE IS ROOM THERE. | Doors open at 7 p.m. Band will give Selections 7 to 8 p.m.

Blacksmith's in Steward Street, 1966

Bulpitt's

Thos. Upton & Sons,

Glass Merchants

20, CAMBRIDGE ST.
BIRMINGHAM

Largest stock in the Midlands of Glass Ware for private and hotel use.

Tel.: MIDland 1850

To Celebrate the
Chamberlain Anniversary

We are giving away 200,000 Picture Post Cards, and every Purchaser of a Cycle during July, 1906 will be presented with a . . .

Chamberlain Lamp

and a

Chamberlain Bell. .

PASKELLS' 162-5 Spring Hill.

(Birmingham's largest Cycle Dealers.)

Phone : MIDland 0397

Removals :: Furniture Transport

●

Shepherd's Garage

(Proprietor : C. Shepherd)

●

41 & 43, Grosvenor Street West
Ladywood, Birmingham, 16

THE SHOPS OF RYLAND STREET

Wheeler's, Greengrocers, 123 Ryland Street - Rabbits were 9d. each and skinned while you waited

Stephen Weston, Butcher, 121 Ryland Street

Mordin and Surrell, Haberdashery, 57 Ryland Street

"Doris", Hat shop - Sold real velour hats for 9s. 11d

Mortimors - Charged batteries for radio's - 6d

Vickers, Confectioners, 41 Ryland Street

Treadwells, Cobbler, 6 Ryland Street

Johnson's, Greengrocers, 11 Ryland Street

Ryland Arms, Public House - Dorothy Compton used to play the accordion here

Stoddards - Sold pigs feet, hot!

Denton's Coffee Shop, 98 Ryland Street

Arthur Pettit, 119 Ryland Street - This was a second-hand shop who sold old bedsteads, prams, etc. He also "lent" out old carts for 6d

Dickason, Shopkeeper, 115 Ryland Street - Sweets for 1/2d.in a cone shaped packet, full to the top. Mr. Dickason's funeral was horse driven in those days, and a band marched in front of the funeral. He worked on the trams

Thomas Grater, musical instrument dealer, 37 Ryland Street - Highly polished violins on the wall

Do you remember?

E. GOSCOMBE,

PRACTICAL PLUMBER

AND

HOUSE DECORATOR.

Estimates Free on Application.

220, CAMDEN STREET,

Corner of Icknield Street,

SPRING HILL, BIRMINGHAM.

For Expert Advice

For Guaranteed Repairs

For Civility & Service

consult . . . .

G. & S. Hamilton

*WATCHMAKERS
and JEWELLERS*

292 Monument Road

(Opposite St. John the Evangelist
Church)

ACCOMMODATION FOR 500 NIGHTLY

ARDEN NEW STREET   A.A. R.A.C.

021-643 1029

COBDEN HAGLEY ROAD

021-454 6621

NORFOLK HAGLEY ROAD

021-454 0810

Hotels of Birmingham

UNLICENSED   LUNCH 9/-   CONFERENCES

For a quick enjoyable coffee

Call at the   **WIMPEY BAR**   by the Odeon

Phone: EDG 2400   National Cheques Only

PARRS FURNISHERS

*Repose Superior Interior Sprung Mattresses
Gate-Leg Tables :: Dining Chairs
Specialists in Occasional Furniture
Stockists for B.M.K. Rugs
Ladylove Kitchen Cabinets
Cots, Fireside Chairs
and many other household requirements.*
PARRS—The Shop where you will get personal attention

122, MONUMENT ROAD

LADYWOOD, B'HAM, 16

Bill Landon & Sons Ltd.

HIGH CLASS BATHROOM EQUIPMENT	**THE CROWN**
•	**ICKNIELD PORT ROAD**
SANITARY WARE	**BIRMINGHAM B16 0RB**
•	
WHIRLPOOLS & SHOWERS	Telephone: 0121-456 3637
•	0121-456 1391
BATHROOM FURNITURE	Facsimile: 0121-456 3219

Stockists and Suppliers to the Trade

The Hardware Products Co.

MEMORY HALL WORKS :: CAMBRIDGE ST. :: BIRMINGHAM

MAKERS OF

**PORTABLE BUILDINGS,
MOTOR GARAGES,
POULTRY HOUSES,
GARDEN SHEDS & SEATS.**

Telephone Central 581

126

Do you remember?

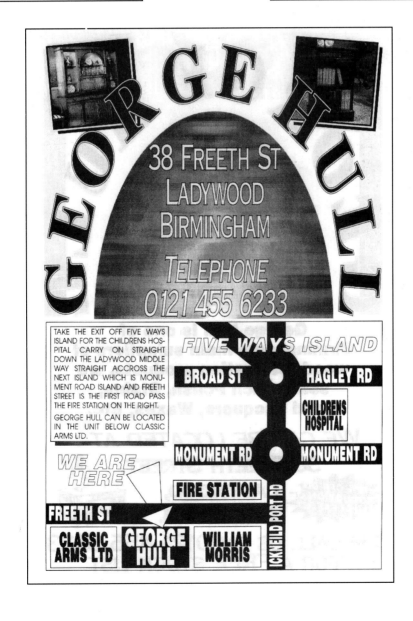

ACKNOWLEDGEMENTS

I would like to thank all the people who have made the publishing of this book possible. They have been kind enough to loan me photographs, taken the trouble to let me write of their memories of an area that really needs to be remembered.

My Dad
Ray James
Phil Trentham
Nellie Fear
Helen Butcher
Mr. Hickman
Mrs. Hurst
Sunday Mercury
Davenports
Birmingham Reference Library
Dr. Carl Chinn
Dennis Pettit
Mecca Ltd.
Barbara Davis
Tina Edwards
Birmingham City Council, Planning and Architectural Department

Dolly Leaver
Ron and Edythe Smith
Laurence Wigley
Albert and Joan Hunt
Paul Cope
Mr. Landon
Rose-Marie Orme
Birmingham Evening Mail
Diocese of Birmingham
Lloyds TSB Group Archives
Ladywood Community Centre
Lil Walker
Sherborne Rubber
Rystar (Ryland Garage)
Residents of Ladywood

Please forgive any possible omissions. Every effort has been made to include all organisations and individuals involved in the book.